CONTENTS

P9-CEJ-092

Introducing Parakeets

Understanding where parakeets come from and how they live

Parakeets groom their feathers with beak and claw to keep them clean, waterproofed, and in top condition.

This yellow-faced blue parakeet is a popular color variety.

Parakeets (often called budgerigars or budgies) are among the world's favorite and most widely kept cage birds and make good pets for children and the elderly as they are easy to care for and good companions. They are friendly, lively birds and will happily chatter away to each other or to you. A single parakeet, in particular, can become quite attached to its owner. Like any pet, however, a parakeet needs time and attention and will rely on you to feed it and keep its cage clean, as well as for company.

The first pet parakeets

The pet parakeet had a rapid rise to fame. Originally from Australia, the first parakeet pair was brought to Europe by the explorer and naturalist John Gould in 1840. Within 40 years, commercial breeding establishments, accommodating more than 100,000 birds, were already supplying a growing demand for parakeets in Europe.

The original wild parakeet was light green, but by the end of the 19th century, other colour mutations had begun to emerge, which increased the parakeet's appeal. In 1925 the Budgerigar Club (later named the Budgerigar Society) was formed in Britain, which helped bring these birds and their new colours to an even wider audience and the parakeet soon overtook the canary in popularity.

When the first blue parakeets appeared in 1910 at a show in London, they caused a sensation and fetched an astronomical sum.

Today, millions of parakeets are kept as pets, aviary, and exhibition subjects all over the world.

Once tame, your parakeet will be happy to perch on your arm.

A parakeet makes a great pet for a child, but those under about eight years old may prefer a pet they can hold – small birds are easily injured.

WHY KEEP A PARAKEET?

There are many reasons why parakeets are the world's most popular pet bird. They are:
- **Easy to keep** – undemanding in their feeding habits, parakeets are highly adaptable.
- **Relatively long-lived** – unlike other Australian parakeets, budgies will settle well in a cage and can live for eight to ten years or more.
  - **Easy to handle** – although they can nip if handled carelessly, they are not difficult to restrain and are safe even for children to handle. They can also be tamed easily.
  - **Sociable** – they will live happily in a pair or can be kept on their own, provided you give them plenty of your attention.
  - **Entertaining** – parakeets love to climb and play as well as fly.

How Parakeets Live – biology and behavior

One of the best ways to understand your parakeet is to discover something about how it lives in the wild. Although pet parakeets are now all bred from captive stock rather than imported from the wild, they retain many of the behavioral and physical traits of their wild relatives.

In their native Australia, wild parakeets travel in large flocks in search of new feeding grounds.

Life in the wild

Parakeets are members of the parrot family and originally come from Australia, where their wild relatives still live. In their native land, they will fly in large flocks for hundreds of miles across the dry country seeking out water and seeding grasses on which they feed.

Wild parakeets are much smaller than their domesticated relatives – 4in (10cm) from the beak to the tip of the tail, whereas a pet parakeet may measure up to 10in (25cm) in length. They are always light green in colour with yellow heads and black-banded back and wings. This coloration acts as a camouflage, allowing the budgerigars to blend into surrounding trees where they are less likely to be seized by hawks and other hungry predators.

Wild parakeets nest in trees and breed whenever conditions are favourable. This is usually when it rains, so that there are plenty of grass seedlings for the chicks to feed on when they hatch. The young chicks have only six weeks to learn and grow before they migrate with the rest of the flock to find new feeding grounds and escape the fierce heat.

Climbing and flying

In the wild, parakeets get around by both flying and climbing: to cover long distances, they will fly, but for short distances they will use their feet and beaks as climbing aids, appropriate for a life in the treetops.

Caged birds need the encouragement of other birds to use their wings and a single parakeet may not get enough exercise unless you regularly let it out of its cage to fly around (see pages 48–49). In fact, any caged bird needs exercise out of its cage daily if it is to remain fit and healthy.

A pet parakeet will use its feet and beak to climb the bars of its cage.

HOW THE BUDGERIGAR GOT ITS NAME

When Captain James Cook discovered Australia in 1770, he and his crew also discovered immense flocks of brilliant green birds. They asked the Aborigines, in sign language, what these birds were called and the reply came "betcherry-gah." Assuming this was the Aborigine's name for the bird, the settlers called it budgerigar. It was only many years later, when linguists translated the Aborigine language, that they discovered the word actually meant good to eat!

Parakeet behavior

As you spend time watching your new parakeet or parakeets, you will notice various behavior patterns. Understanding what your parakeet is doing and why is important so that you are able to spot quickly if your pet shows signs of becoming ill.

The healthy and normal behavior patterns described opposite should be read in conjunction with the table of disease symptoms on pages 58–59.

BASIC PARAKEET ANATOMY

Crown – barring will extend down the forehead on juveniles.

Beak – used for cracking open seeds, climbing, and preening.

Throat spots – large and round in an adult. Not present in lutinos and albinos.

Breast– the parakeet's body is covered in small contour feathers, which offer protection from cold and rain.

Eyes– parakeets have good color vision and a wide field of vision.

Cere – blue in mature males; brown in mature females.

Cheek patches – violet in all normal varieties.

Nape

Mantle

Wing – the larger feathers at the back of the wings are called flights.

Rump

Feet– a parakeet's claws are hand-like gripping tools.

Tail feathers (retrices)

UNDERSTANDING YOUR PARAKEET

What your parakeet does	What it means
Parakeets offering each other food.	Parakeets will feed each other regurgitated food as a sign of strong affection and a single parakeet may try to feed you. A male, in particular, may even to try to feed its mirror or a toy in its cage.
A parakeet is quieter than usual and is losing a lot of feathers.	Parakeets molt regularly and may be quieter at this time. Feather-plucking, on the other hand, can be a result of stress or boredom and is a hard habit to break.
Two parakeets are preening each other.	Another signal of strong affection. A single parakeet may even try to nibble your hair, eyebrows, or ears. Parakeets will also preen themselves, of course.
Your parakeet leans towards you with its beak.	Parakeets use their beaks to investigate things. Your parakeet is probably checking that your finger is a safe perch rather than trying to bite you.
Your new pet spends a lot of its time on the floor of its cage.	This is normal for a young bird – chicks are not used to perching for long periods of time. However, if your parakeet is not a youngster, or if it does not hop up on the perch when you approach, this may be a sign of illness.
Your parakeet is shredding the sand sheets on the bottom of its cage.	This destructive behaviour is normal at breeding time for hen birds, who may even lay eggs.
A cock parakeet is tapping at the perch while singing.	This is typical parakeet display behaviour. A cock's eyes may also appear whiter for a period.

Parakeet Varieties

Colors, wing markings and feather variants

It is virtually impossible to calculate the number of possible parakeet varieties – there are so many that could be produced. Yet, despite their varied appearances, all parakeet belong to the same species, Melopsittacus undulatus. *The primary mutations – as distinct from the various combinations of these – can be divided into three categories: color varieties, wing markings, and feather variants.*

very pale, for example. Pied parakeet have variegated or banded markings, while another rare variety, the rainbow, combines green, yellow, and blue together.

Crests and tufts

Apart from the various colors and patterns, there has been only one successful variation on the basic parakeet "model:" the crested parakeet, which occurs in three different forms (see page 22).

The lutino, with its pure yellow coloration, red eyes and lack of black markings, was one of the first color varieties to be developed and is still very popular today.

This cobalt spangle cock shows the characteristic light feathers with attractive dark edging.

The colors

There are no blacks, browns, reds or pinks to be found in parakeet, just blue, green, white and yellow, but these extend over a wide range of shades and come in various combinations. Parakeets with black wing markings and throat spots – like the wild type – are known as normals and come in different shades of greens and blues depending on the amount of dark pigment (melanin) present.

The absence of melanin produces the lutino (see page 16), while the albino parakeet (see pages 16–17) has neither dark nor yellow pigment.

Different markings

The black throat spots and barring on the wings and back of the head of normal varieties may be diluted as well absent (as in lutinos and albinos). In cinnamons, these markings are brown rather than black, in the rare graywings they are gray, and in clearwings they are

Parakeet Colors

The two main colors of parakeets are blue and green and each comes in three shades. In these six normal varieties, the wing markings and throat spots are black and the face is white in the blue series and yellow in the green series.

All normal series parakeets have violet cheek patches.

Green series

Light green is the normal coloration of the budgerigar and has been widely used in the development of other mutations. (The mating of two light greens usually gives rise to various other colors in the chicks.) The emergence of the dark factor – the gene that darkens the coloration of the parakeet – in the early 20th century, meant that it was possible to obtain greens of other shades: dark green and olive green. Pairing dark greens together is the most versatile option in terms of color production as, in theory, all three shades of green should be represented in the chicks.

Normal Light Green *This is the coloration of the wild parakeet, though the pet variety is much larger than its wild relative.*

Normal Dark Green *This shade is between the light and olive green. There is also a violet form of the dark green.*

Normal Gray

Gray parakeets

The addition of gray to the colors has a different effect in green and blue series parakeets. In the green series, the green becomes almost khaki (see the Dominant Pied Gray Green on page 17), while in the blue series, the gray covers up all the blue and the bird appears light, mid or dark gray.

Normal Olive Green

Blue series

Blue parakeets have been popular since the first ones appeared in 1910. As with the green series, the presence of the dark factor has led to three different shades of blue varieties. Sky blue was the original blue parakeet to appear; cobalts have one dark factor present in their genetic make-up, while mauves have two.

Normal Sky Blue

Normal Cobalt

Normal (Visual) Violet

Violet, which should ideally be a deep purplish shade, is considered a color in its own right and is not part of the blue series. The violet mutation can also be combined with green series parakeets to give rise to violet dark greens, which are distinguishable from the normal variety by their darker and often more yellowish coloration.

The violet coloration can also be featured on dominant and recessive pieds (see page 17) and in combination with many different forms of markings.

Normal Mauve The blues series equivalent of the olive green – both are double dark factor. Mauve parakeets first appeared in about 1924.

Normal (Visual) Violet *Although this parakeet looks blue, the Violet is a variety in its own right and is not part of the normal blue series.*

YELLOW-FACED BLUES

Although the original (normal) blue series birds have a white head, yellow-faced blues have been in existence since the late 1930s and are now very popular. There are two forms of yellow-faced blue parakeets, which were originally described as types I and II, type I having lighter coloration. Today, the deepest colored individuals are sometimes known as golden-faced. The yellow-faced mutation can appear on blue parakeets of all shades.

It used to be thought impossible to combine yellow and blue on one bird, but the yellow-faced characteristic has proved to be dominant.

Eyes are dark red in color rather than the normal black.

The cere of this cock is light purplish rather than the blue of a normal series bird.

Cheek patches are white rather than the violet of normal series parakeets.

Lutino *Its attractive rich yellow coloration continues to ensure the popularity of this variety.*

Lutino

The deep rich yellow lutino is a justifiably popular bird. Although lutinos were bred on several occasions in the late 19th century, the mutation was not finally established until the 1930s. As the green series equivalent of the albino, lutino parakeets sometimes show some green in their coloration but in exhibition birds, this is considered a show fault.

Albino

Albino parakeets lack any dark or yellow pigment in their genetic make-up. They do have blue pigment, but this should not be visible: albinos should appear pure white, with reddish eyes, pink legs and a pale yellowish beak. Cocks have light purplish rather than blue ceres. The albino is less common than the lutino and tends to be relatively small.

Albino *This pure white parakeet shows no undesirable shades of blue in its plumage.*

Dominant Pied Gray Green

Pied parakeets

Pied parakeets have a variable and sporadic absence of dark pigment over the body and so can vary widely in appearance. In green series birds, clear areas show as yellow; in blue series birds they are white. Dominant and recessive pieds are distinguishable from each other visually as well as genetically and both can be bred in the full range of colors.

Dominant pieds resemble normals, with throat spots and cheek flashes and black eyes with white irises, but they have an area of clear plumage. In some, known as banded pieds, this clear area forms a distinctive band across the front of the body (see the bottom two parakeets in the picture on page 10).

Recessive pieds are more slender with a larger area of clear plumage and have plum-colored eyes with no visible irises.

Recessive Pied Sky Blue

The cock has a purplish-mauve rather than blue cere.

The number of throat spots ranges from one to a full complement of six.

Wing Markings

The varieties that follow are distinguished by the color, type, and extent of the markings on their wings. All these varieties, with the exception of the lacewing (see pages 20–21), which looks like an albino or lutino with cinnamon markings, can be combined with any of the colors on the previous pages and, in some cases, with each other, as in Opaline Cinnamon Sky Blue, for example.

Cinnamon

The cinnamon mutation reduces the amount of melanin, changing black markings – the bars on the back of the head and wings and the throat spots – to brown. The eyes are a deep shade of plum red. The body color also becomes a more delicate shade than in the normal variety.

These two birds show the black wing markings of normal budgies, which are modified in the other varieties shown here.

markings varies. The flight feathers and tail are similarly marked and the throat spots have pale centres.

Spangle

One of the most recent parakeet varieties to be recorded, the spangle has become very well known and popular since it was first reported in 1977 in Australia. The plumage over the wings is light in the centre, with attractive dark edging around individual feathers. The depth of the

tip
Provide supplements during a molt

Whatever color your parakeet's feathers, they will eventually be molted. The molt is when your bird is at its most vulnerable so supplement its diet with an iron and vitamin-mineral tonic until the new feathers emerge.

Opaline

Opalines arose in Australia, Scotland, and Belgium during the 1930s and are now both commonly available and popular. In an opaline parakeet, the barring on the head is less prominent than in the normal variety and in a well-marked individual there is a V-shaped area on the back free of markings. The darker plumage is confined solely to the wings.

1: *Cinnamon Violet.* 2: *Opaline Light Green.*
3: *Spangle Grey.*

Clearwings

This is the collective name for parakeets in which the wing markings are virtually free of melanin, making them paler than graywings. In blue series birds, this mutation alters the coloration on the wings so that they become virtually white and these parakeetss are known as whitewings. In the green series, the yellow wing markings create an attractive contrast with the green body coloration, especially in the darker green birds. Pairing these so-called yellow-wings with whitewings can improve their coloration.

1: Whitewing Sky Blue. 2: Yellow-wing Light Green. 3: Lacewing White. 4: Lacewing Yellow. 5: German Fallow.

Graywing

Here, the normal black markings are diluted to gray, and the body coloration may also be slightly paler than in the normal variety. It is possible that this variety may have arisen as early as 1918, but it is now rare.

Lacewing

This is one of several parakeet mutations to have emerged since World War II (in 1950). Others are the dark-eyed clear (1947), crested (1955), Australian pied (1952), spangle (1977) and, most recently, the anthracite (2003).

Lacewings, which are also quite rare, were originally believed to be the result

3

4

5

of introducing cinnamon blood but are now accepted as a separate variety. The rare lacewing mutation affects red-eyed parakeets, creating a lace-like pattern of pale brown markings on their wings, with throat spots and colored cheek patches also being present.

Fallow

In the early 1930s there were three distinct fallow mutations, occurring in the USA, Germany, and Australia respectively. The German strain is now the best known, but all are rare. Fallow parakeets have brown throat spots and wing markings (similar to those of cinnamons), red eyes and a paler body colour than normal varieties.

Feather Variants and Rare Varieties

If you are looking for something a bit different, you may want to try to find a crested or tufted variety – though these are not that common – or explore some of the other rarer or newer varieties.

In addition to crested parakeets, other feather variants also exist, but most are not only rare but also considered to be genetic defects. Among such are the long-flighted parakeet, Japanese heavenly body, which has abnormal tufted feathering on its back and wings as well as on its head, and feather-dusters, whose feathers continue to grow to the extent that they are no longer able to see.

Full-circular Crested Light Green

Tufted Gray Green

Crests and tufts

There are three distinct forms of crested or tufted parakeet. The full-circular has an even crest positioned centrally on the head, reaching down to, but not obscuring, the eyes and cere. The half-circular is similar in appearance, but the crest extends only forwards from a point above the eyes towards the beak. The third form of crest is the tufted, where the plumage above the cere is raised to form a tuft.

Rare varieties

Not all parakeet color and marking varieties have been successfully established and new ones are appearing all the time. Some of those shown on previous pages are categorized by The Budgerigar Society as rare, including the mauve, graywing, lacewing, and fallow (see pages 15 and 20–21). Some other attractive, but rare, varieties are shown here.

Slate A good slate should have all the features of a normal parakeet but a pure slate blue colour, whose depth should vary in darkness according to whether the bird is basically sky blue, cobalt or mauve.

Dilute (gray yellow) *This was the first parakeet mutation, or color variation, and the gene that brings it about is recessive to all others. The gray yellow has a dull mustard yellow body, with no green coloring, and pale gray cheek patches.*

Texas Clearbody *A new variety, the Texas Clearbody was first exported from the USA to the UK in 1989. It differs from the normal colors in that the flight feathers are pale gray instead of black and the body color has less than half the normal intensity of color.*

Rainbow *This variety is a mixture of many characteristics in one. The Parakeet Society recognizes these colourful parakeets as yellow-faced (or golden-faced) opaline whitewing blues.*

Housing Parakeets

Choosing and positioning a suitable cage or aviary

Before you buy your first parakeet or parakeets you will need to plan carefully where you are going to house them, prepare suitable accommodations, and buy all the necessary equipment. Parakeets are active birds and will need enough space to fly, climb and play, so, as with any pet, choose the largest cage you can afford. Birds kept indoors will also need to have somewhere safe where they can fly around (see pages 48–49).

Cage or aviary?

Most parakeet owners start with an indoor cage suitable for one or two birds and this is certainly the easiest and least expensive option. Once you have a bit more experience – and provided you have the space –

you may want to think about building or buying an outdoor aviary. This is obviously a more costly option and the birds will not become as tame as an indoor pet but you will be able to house many more birds in an aviary.

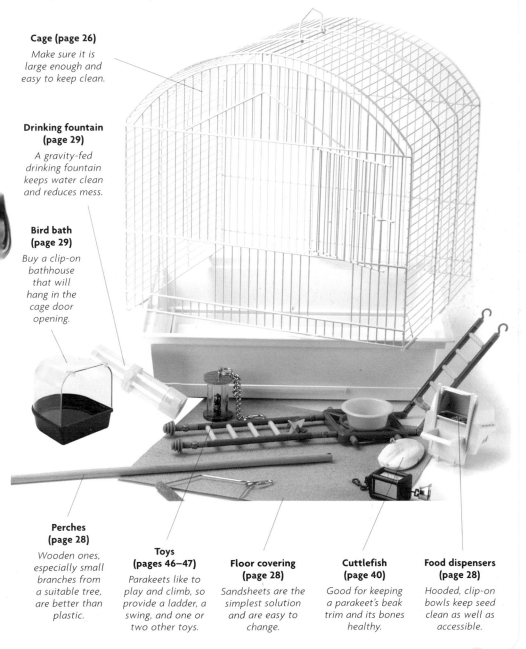

ESSENTIAL EQUIPMENT

'Starter kits' for keeping budgies often include food and water containers, ladders, perches, and toys as well as the cage itself. Make sure that you have all the following:

Cage (page 26)

Make sure it is large enough and easy to keep clean.

Drinking fountain (page 29)

A gravity-fed drinking fountain keeps water clean and reduces mess.

Bird bath (page 29)

Buy a clip-on bathhouse that will hang in the cage door opening.

Perches (page 28)

Wooden ones, especially small branches from a suitable tree, are better than plastic.

Toys (pages 46–47)

Parakeets like to play and climb, so provide a ladder, a swing, and one or two other toys.

Floor covering (page 28)

Sandsheets are the simplest solution and are easy to change.

Cuttlefish (page 40)

Good for keeping a parakeet's beak trim and its bones healthy.

Food dispensers (page 28)

Hooded, clip-on bowls keep seed clean as well as accessible.

The Cage – housing parakeets indoors

The most important consideration in choosing a cage is its size. Many cages function as small, cramped prisons, particularly if a parakeet is not allowed out. Choose the largest one you can afford and accommodate, but, in any case, it should not be smaller than 20in (50cm) long, 12in (30cm) wide and 18in (45cm) high. No matter how large the cage, your parakeet will need daily flying time outside it to stay fit and healthy.

Horizontal bars will be easier for parakeets to climb than vertical ones. They should be no wider apart than 0.5in (12mm) or a parakeet could trap its head between them.

ideally, the bars should be horizontal rather than vertical to allow your pet climbing exercise. Avoid plastic or wooden cage bars, which a parakeet will soon chew through. Metal (brass or chome-plated) bars must be free of rust, as parakeets will nibble them. Resin-coated bars won't rust and are easier to clean.

A good cage design will have a sliding tray in the base in which to lay a sandsheet. This makes cleaning the cage much easier.

A pull-out tray in the cage base will make daily floor cleaning a simple task.

Cage design

The design of the cage is also important. It should provide enough flying space (so length is more important than height) and,

Siting the cage

Parakeets are sociable birds and need company, particularly if you have a single bird. However, they won't like constant noisy activity, nor the kitchen, where fumes and temperature changes will affect them. Remember that your pet will need daily exercise outside its cage, so it makes sense to choose a room that will be safe for a free-flying parakeet (see also pages 48–49).

Make sure the cage is not in direct sunlight or drafts. A position near a window, door, or radiator (or other heat source) should be avoided. A corner location where the cage will not be knocked is often the best option.

Your parakeet will feel safer if it is in a higher position. Place the cage on a high sturdy shelf or table or use a cage stand in order to bring your parakeet to your eye-level.

If you want to use a cage stand, make sure you choose a suitable cage for hanging.

Your parakeets will feel more secure if their cage is no lower than your eye-level.

Perches

A new cage will probably have ready-made perches in it, but if these are plastic, replace them right away, as they are uncomfortable for most parakeets. Wooden dowelling, usually 0.5in (12.5mm) diameter, is commonly used for perches, but as it is of a constant diameter, a parakeet's feet can develop pressure sores.

The best option is to use natural wood. You can cut branches from a variety of trees — sycamore and apple are particularly good — but make sure that the wood has not been treated with preservatives. Cut branches so that they fit comfortably across the cage without distorting the bars. You may be able to use the plastic tips supplied with dowelling perches to attach the branches to the cage bars.

Concrete perches are another option and will file claws and beaks, preventing them from becoming overgrown.

A perch at either end of the cage will encourage your parakeet to fly but make sure perches are not so close to the ends of the cage that your parakeet's tail rubs against the cage bars. Avoid positioning perches directly above each other or the lower one will become soiled.

Natural wood perches are best for a budgie's feet.

Floor covering

Sandsheets, which slot into a pull-out tray in the base of the cage, are the easiest — and most widely used — option for keeping the base of the cage clean, but some owners use loose sand or newspapers instead.

Food and water containers

Food and water need to be protected from fouling, so covered containers are best and ones that clip on to the bars of the cage often come with the cage. Avoid positioning them directly under perches.

The best solution for providing your parakeet with clean water is a

Provide seed easily and hygienically for your budgie in a hooded, clip-on bowl.

gravity-fed drinking fountain, which can be clipped to the cage bars. You will probably need to buy this separately.

Bath-time

Regular bathing is essential to keep a parakeet's feathers clean and healthy. You can place a saucer of water on the floor of the cage, removing it immediately after use, but this can create quite a mess. A better option is a detachable bathhouse that is designed to hang in the cage door opening. Choose one with a grooved floor so that your parakeet doesn't slip. If your bird doesn't enjoy bathing, you can spray it with an mister occasionally.

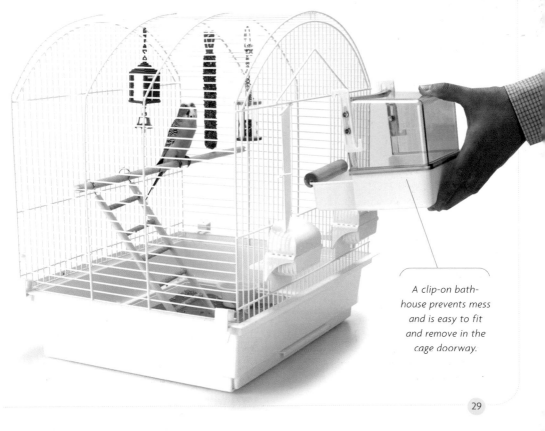

A clip-on bath-house prevents mess and is easy to fit and remove in the cage doorway.

The Aviary – housing parakeets outside

Housing parakeets in an outdoor aviary is clearly a more expensive option, but is worthwhile if you want to keep several birds. Many companies now offer aviaries in kit form, which can be delivered to your house and put together in the garden. However, you will still need to prepare adequate foundations and, ideally, lay a concrete floor.

A basic aviary

The simplest aviary design will consist of an outer flight, constructed from wire netting on a wooden framework, and a weatherproof shelter where the birds are fed and can go at night or during bad weather. Birds will need access from one to the other via a hatch and you will need a door. The shelter should also have a safety porch to prevent birds escaping when you go in to feed them. This can be a simple mesh-covered structure attached to the door of the shelter. A window in the side of the shelter will enable you to see the birds without going inside.

Aviary furnishings

You will need to supply your aviary birds with perches, a bird bath, and swings and ladders for play in the flight. Provide drinking fountains and food containers in the shelter. Food hoppers will prevent food wastage and soiling and will deter rodents, as will storing food in tightly sealed containers.

Branches from a small tree provide these parakeets with plenty of perching places.

Provide a perch or landing platform on either side of the access hole. A sliding cover over the hole would enable you to confine birds in the flight or shelter.

SITING AN AVIARY

Ask yourself the following questions before you decide on the best spot for an aviary.

- Can it be seen from the road? (Parakeets may provide a target for thieves and car headlights may disturb birds at night.)
- Will noise from the birds disturb you or your neighbors?
- Is the proposed spot far enough away from car noise and fumes?
- Is the spot suitably sheltered and adequately drained?
- Do you have, or can you create, easy (mud-free) access to the aviary from the house?
- Will there be room to extend the aviary if you later wish to do so?
- Is the site suitably level? (Preparing foundations will be more difficult on a sloping site.)
- Do you need building permits?

This simple aviary is in a sheltered spot away from the house and provides plenty of flying space and perching places for its occupants.

tip

Deter cats

Prevent cats from perching on top of the aviary by extending strands of very thin mesh on supports around the roof.

Buying Your Parakeet

Where and when to buy and how to choose a healthy bird

Before you start visiting pet shops to seek out your new pet, you will need to decide whether you are going to buy one bird or two. Parakeets need company and will need either to live as a pair or to spend lots of time with you. Although a single bird may become closer to you – and is more likely to learn to talk – than two living together, it would be unfair on a pet parakeet to keep it on its own if you are out of the house for most of the day.

Male or female?

Both males and females make good pets. If you decide to keep two birds together, two cocks will present fewer difficulties than a pair and are likely to be less quarrelsome than two hens. Unfortunately, though it is easy to sex adult parakeets by cere color, this does not develop until the birds are mature.

When to buy

Baby parakeets are ready to leave the nest at about six weeks old. The best age to buy a parakeet is when it is between six and twelve weeks old. Immature birds, under three months old, are distinguishable by their

SPOTTING A YOUNG PARAKEET

Eyes are dark and lack the white irises of most adult parakeets.

The barring on the head extends down as far as the cere.

The cere is mauve in color on youngsters of both sexes.

The spots that form the mask are small and slightly elongated.

SEXING ADULT PARAKEETS

Males (cocks) of most varieties have a blue cere. (In some varieties, including albinos, lutinos and recessive pieds, the cere is purplish.)

In female parakeets (hens), the cere is invariably brown in color.

dark eyes, barring on the forehead (in blue and green series birds) and pale ceres and by their tendency to huddle together and spend more time on the floor. Young birds will be slightly more expensive to buy, but they will be easier to tame.

Once a parakeet has reached maturity, it is virtually impossible to age it accurately unless it has been fitted with a breeder's closed ring, which will be marked with the year of hatching.

BUYING AVIARY STOCK

You may be able to purchase the complete stock of someone who is selling out, usually at a competitive price, but this means you will need to take all their birds. Alternatively, you can buy parakeets in ones and twos from different sources, but obtaining birds in this way heightens the risk of introducing disease or parasites to an aviary. It is therefore advisable to house all new arrivals separately for at least two weeks.

The Right Bird – choosing healthy parakeets

It is important to choose carefully – not only the individual parakeet, but also your retailer. Most pet shops sell a good selection of parakeets, as well as cages, food, etc, but they will vary in their knowledge of their stock and the environment in which they are kept. It is not a good idea to buy even an apparently healthy bird from a retailer where cages are cramped and dirty. Feel free to visit a few outlets and ask questions of the staff. Look carefully at how the birds are being kept. They should be well housed, well tended, and tame.

Selecting a healthy bird

Having found a good retailer, you are ready to select your new pet. There is little difference in terms of temperament between the different varieties (though recessive pieds can sometimes be more timid than others), so your main job will be to find a healthy one.

WHAT TO LOOK FOR

Eyes should look bright and alert.

There should be no discharge from the nostrils.

Plumage should be sleek.

Check that the beak is trim and does not overhang.

Wing and tail feathers should be undamaged.

Breast should be plump: if you can feel the ribs, the bird is too thin.

Feet should be clean and have four normal toes.

Vent area should be clean.

tip

Don't be tempted by a neglected bird

Never pick a parakeet because you feel sorry it. Remember that scruffiness isn't cute, it's a sign of ill-health.

34

Start by looking at how it behaves. It should appear alert and tame and, if it is housed with others, should be sociable. If you see a bird you like the look of, ask the retailer to let you examine it more closely.

Your parakeet will be safest transported home in a small box with air holes.

Having somewhere to hide will help your new pet recover from the stress of moving home.

Taking your parakeet home

When you have chosen your parakeet, the retailer should provide you with a small cardboard box in which to transport it home. The journey will be stressful for your new pet, so go straight home, carry the box carefully in your hands, and protect it from jolts. On a cold day, wrap your coat loosely around it, but make sure you keep air holes clear.

When you arrive home

Pop the carrying box into the cage and open one end of it. When the parakeet is safely sitting on its perch, you can remove the box from the cage. Make sure your parakeet has fresh food and water available, cover half its cage so that it has somewhere to hide, then leave it alone to settle in.

Caring for Your Parakeet

Enjoying your parakeet and keeping it healthy

Parakeets are not demanding to look after – their diet is simple and a cage is easy to clean out. But to enjoy your parakeet and keep it happy and healthy, you will need to give it lots of attention. It is a good idea to keep a record of when you carry out maintenance tasks (see page 52) and of any changes in your bird's appearance and behavior. This will help you to identify quickly any problems that may arise.

Settling in

During the first few weeks, your new parakeet will need time to adjust to its new surroundings. Take extra care to ensure that the house is quiet and peaceful to protect your parakeet from shock. Avoid slamming doors, loud music or television, and shouting as well as sudden changes is light intensity.

Introducing a
second parakeet

If you want to keep two parakeets together, it is always best to buy them both at the same time and from the same source. Although sociable by nature, your pet parakeet may not appreciate the sudden arrival of another bird in its cage, and new introductions should be carried out carefully to prevent distress and fighting.

Keep the new bird in a separate cage for two to four weeks to make sure that it is healthy and to help it adjust to its new surroundings. Treat the new parakeet with a special spray (available from your pet shop or vet) to kill any mites or feather lice it may be carrying.

Keep the parakeets within sight and sound of each other after the third week, to give them a chance to get to know each other from a distance.

Two parakeets will not be as easy to train as one. If you don't buy them together, you will need to introduce the birds to each other carefully.

PARAKEETS AND OTHER PETS

Other pets can be a danger to a parakeet. Although with time and training a dog and a parakeet may learn to co-exist, it is unfair to expect a cat to ignore its natural instincts when faced with a parakeet flying around. Make sure that the cage is out of reach of other pets and that they are shut out of the room before you let your parakeet out of its cage.

Feeding – providing a balanced diet

Most of your parakeet's nutritional needs will be supplied by a seed mix, which you can buy from any pet store – make sure you choose one specially designed for parakeets. Various types are available and should include canary seed, millet, red rape, linseed, and niger. Some also contain vitamin and mineral supplements.

Parakeets need to eat little and often. As a rough guide, provide one and a half to two teaspoons of seed per day. Parakeets nibble off the husk of the seeds, eating only the kernel. They won't hunt under the husks for fresh seeds, so you will need to remove the husks periodically. If you are supplying the seed in a pot, simply blow away the husks; if you are using a food hopper, put your finger over the hole, take the top off and tip out the little dish. Then put it all back together. When the bowls are nearly empty, tip the last few seeds out and refill with fresh seed.

Make sure that you regularly remove husks from the seed container so that your parakeet can find its food.

SPROUTED SEEDS

Your parakeet will enjoy eating sprouted seeds and they are easy to prepare. Simply soak a spoonful of seed mix in a saucer of water and leave it in a warm place for 24 hours. Rinse and leave to soak for a further 24–48 hours, by which time the seeds should have begun to sprout. Rinse again and discard any moldy sprouts before serving.

tip

Buy food in small quantities
Parakeet seed and other food will get stale if stored for long periods. Keep seed in airtight jars to prevent contamination.

A good parakeet seed mix will include canary seed, millet, red rape, linseed, and niger.

A gravity-fed water bottle will help keep water clean.

Water

Parakeets do not drink large quantities of water, but fresh water must be available to them at all times. Change the water every day to keep it clean and free from bacteria. Tap water is best unless you live in an area where tap water is heavily chlorinated, in which case leave it to

Provide your parakeet with grit in a separate container.

stand in a bowl for a few hours to allow the chlorine to disperse. If you have any doubts about the quality of your water, use non-carbonated mineral water instead.

Digesting food

Parakeets use their beaks to remove the husks from seeds but the seed is then swallowed whole. The seed is broken down in the gizzard with the help of grit particles and so it is important that you supply grit regularly to your parakeet. Fine grit for the purpose is sold by pet stores. Offer your parakeet a small dish of grit for one day each month.

Fresh food

Fruit and greens will help to keep your parakeet healthy and should comprise about a quarter of its daily diet. Many different types of greens are suitable, including salad greens (but not lettuce), dandelion, chickweed, parsley, spinach, freshly sprouted seeds (see page 38), and seeding grasses.

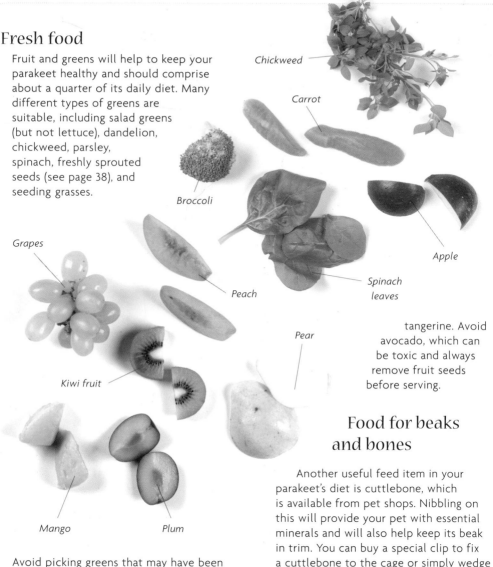

Chickweed

Carrot

Broccoli

Apple

Grapes

Spinach leaves

Peach

Pear

Kiwi fruit

Mango

Plum

tangerine. Avoid avocado, which can be toxic and always remove fruit seeds before serving.

Food for beaks and bones

Another useful feed item in your parakeet's diet is cuttlebone, which is available from pet shops. Nibbling on this will provide your pet with essential minerals and will also help keep its beak in trim. You can buy a special clip to fix a cuttlebone to the cage or simply wedge it between the bars. A mineral or iodine block will also help to keep your bird's beak trim and its bones healthy.

Avoid picking greens that may have been contaminated with pesticides and wash all fruit and vegetables thoroughly before offering them to your parakeet. Feed only a small piece at a time in a separate bowl or wedge a piece of carrot or apple between the cage bars.

Fresh fruit makes a good treat too: try apple, grape, guava, kiwi fruit, mango, melon, nectarine, orange, peach, pear, pomegranate, plum, strawberry or

tip ***Make sure fresh food is fresh***
Never offer your parakeet tired, wilting greens or over-ripe fruit and remove any uneaten food daily.

Treats and titbits

As with any pet – and indeed humans – parakeets are best fed healthy treats, such as a piece of fruit. It is never a good idea to feed your parakeet treats intended for humans. At best they will do no good and at worst they may be dangerous – sticky foods, for example, can clog the beak, causing distress. Your pet shop will have a variety of other treats you can offer your pet, such as seed bells and fruit

Millet sprays provide exercise for feet and beaks but are fattening, so make sure they are only an occasional treat.

sticks, but as these are bound together with honey or similar agents, they are best given no more often than once a month.

One treat your parakeet will certainly enjoy is a millet spray. However, as millet will already form part of your parakeet's seed mix and it is fattening, you should avoid offering your parakeet more than one millet spray a week.

Most parakeets also enjoy snacks such as salads, cheese, egg, or yogurt, but don't overdo dairy products or sugar, and make sure you remove any uneaten portions of food promptly.

A cuttlebone will provide calcium, beak exercise and hours of amusement for your parakeet.

Taming – getting to know each other

Parakeets don't like being picked up, but if you train it from a youngster, your parakeet will be happy to perch on your finger or even on your shoulder or head. Most recently fledged parakeets will be naturally tame, although they may be somewhat nervous at first.

Parakeets are also often good mimics, particularly those that live on their own without access to a mirror in the cage (which may take the place of another bird or its owner in a parakeet's affections). If you have a single parakeet, and are prepared to spend lots of time talking to it, it can learn to repeat words or even phrases.

First approaches

During the first few weeks, be particularly careful to approach your parakeet's cage quietly. Spend time talking gently to your new pet every day so that it becomes used to the sound of your voice and learns to associate your approach with food and company. Although your parakeet won't understand the words you speak to it, your tone of voice will reassure it if you speak calmly and quietly.

Try to avoid staring at your parakeet, which is likely to be quite nervous when it first comes to live with you. Put your hand flat against the cage as you talk to your pet and look away. It will soon become accustomed to your presence. Once your parakeet has got used to you, you can begin to hand-tame it.

tip

Be patient

Birds are naturally nervous and training a parakeet takes time, so be consistent and regular with your training sessions.

Look away from the cage while you get to know your parakeet so that you don't alarm it.

HAND-TAMING YOUR PARAKEET

1 Slowly reach into the cage with some food in your hand. You can offer some seed in the palm of your hand or a spinach leaf or piece of fruit or vegetable. Eventually – and it may take some time – your parakeet will feel confident enough to feed from your hand.

2 Once your parakeet is completely comfortable with hand-feeding, you can begin to gently stroke its breast and lower abdomen. Move slowly and if your pet moves away, try this again another time.

3 The next stage is to move your finger towards your parakeet's feet and encourage it to step onto your finger. Keep your forefinger parallel to its perch and your parakeet will come to view your finger as a safe perch.

4 Once your parakeet is confident enough to perch on your finger, you can start training it to come to your hand when called and to lift it, perched on your hand, from its cage.

How to hold a parakeet

Training your parakeet to become hand-tame so that it will come and perch on your finger when you give the command, is by far the best way of handling it. However, there will be times when you need to pick your parakeet up and it is important that you know how to do this without harming your parakeet or it nipping you.

If you are right-handed, keep your parakeet's back and wings restrained in the palm of your left hand, shifting its head so that it lies between the first and second fingers of your hand. Use your thumb and other fingers to encircle the front of the parakeet's body.

Held in this way, the parakeet will be restrained and unable to bite, yet most of its body will be easily accessible, including the wings. Ask your pet shop staff to demonstrate the technique if you are in any doubt.

The secret with teaching your parakeet to talk is constant repetition and lots of patience!

Hold your parakeet firmly but be careful not to grip its neck too tightly with your fingers or you may interfere with its breathing.

Teaching a parakeet to talk

Constant and consistent repetition will enable your parakeet to learn its name and some simple commands. For example, you can say 'Home!' to tell your parakeet that it is time to go back into its cage. Repeat this every time you want it to return to its cage and reward its return, however slow, with a favourite tidbit and it will eventually learn to obey the command.

A FAMOUS TALKING PARAKEET

One of the most famous talking parakeets ever known, named Sparkie Williams, learned eight complete nursery rhymes, nearly 360 phrases and had a complete vocabulary of more than 550 words. Shortly before his death in 1962, Sparkie became a recording star, selling 20,000 copies of his record and featuring in several radio programmes.

Your parakeet may also learn to say its own name as well as other words. Keep repeating one word over and over again until it mimics you. Once it has learned that word, try another and then build up short phrases. Don't be disappointed if your pet never learns to speak, however; although single parakeets are generally easier to teach to talk than those living together, some never learn to speak.

Teach your parakeet where it lives

Some owners have taught their parakeets to repeat their address or a phone number. If you do so, your parakeet can be reunited with you if it escapes.

Once tame, your parakeet will be as happy perching on your head or shoulder as on your finger.

Exercise – providing suitable playthings

Parakeets are naturally inquisitive and playful and will enjoy the stimulation of toys in their cage. Your pet shop will have a large number of parakeet toys available, but although it is tempting to buy lots of different ones, don't over-clutter the cage. Limit toys to two or three and swap them out periodically to keep your parakeet's interest alive. Avoid designs that could be easily destroyed or that have any sharp projections. Simple ones often prove the most popular as well as the safest and easiest to clean.

Some ladders hook onto perches.

As well as giving your parakeet hours of amusement, a ladder will provide it with useful foot exercise.

Ladders and swings

Parakeets enjoy climbing on the bars of their cage, but they also like to have a ladder to climb. Some cages come equipped with ladders and swings as well as perches, but you can buy them separately, too. Some ladders are jointed in the middle and incorporate toys that a parakeet can turn with its beak.

This ladder is jointed in the middle and incorporates a food bowl as well as other toys.

Mirrors, bells and other toys

A wide range of other toys for parakeets will be available in your pet store: some fix onto a perch, others hang from the cage bars and some can go on the cage floor.

Mirrors often prove popular, especially with parakeets that live on their own. The parakeet's reflection will act as a companion for it. Your pet will happily chat away to it for hours, but a parakeet with a mirror is less likely to learn to talk. Sometimes a parakeet may attempt to feed its reflection and even regurgitate seed. If this develops into a regular habit, you should remove the mirror for several weeks.

You can buy a wide variety of hanging toys for your parakeet to make its life more interesting.

If you choose a bell for your parakeet's cage, make sure it has no sharp edges. Bear in mind, too, that your parakeet can create a lot of noise with it!

FRESH AIR

In summer you can give your parakeet an outing by taking its cage outside for a while. Sunshine is good for your pet, but never leave the cage unattended in reach of other pets or in direct sun. Many parakeets will also enjoy 10 minutes or so in light rain taking a natural bath.

Make some toys

Empty cotton reels tied together with strong string makes a good toy. Your parakeet will also enjoy playing with a fir cone.

Safety Out of the Cage

Parakeets need plenty of exercise, which means that you should allow a caged parakeet flying time outside its cage every day as far as possible. Allow yourself plenty of time for the first occasion you allow your parakeet out of its cage and make sure that doors and windows are shut and that anything dangerous is out of reach. Coax your pet onto your finger and gently withdraw your hand from the cage.

Parakeets are curious and, despite your best efforts, your pet may find some destructive pursuit to engage in, such as plucking a hole in a rug or peeling off wallpaper. Don't scold or punish your parakeet or you will lose its trust. Simply say 'No' and offer a distraction, or pop it back in its cage for a while.

Your parakeet will enjoy flying space and the chance to explore outside its cage, but you can coax it to sit on your finger too.

tip *Set up a climbing tree in the room*
Wedge a sturdy branch firmly into a soil-filled bucket to provide your parakeet with some perches while it is out of the cage. This will also help you to keep the rest of the room free of droppings.

SAFETY IN THE HOME

Before letting your parakeet loose in the room, make sure that you do the following.
- Close all doors and windows and block off any other escape routes.
- Remove hazards such as poisonous plants, potential traps (pots, open drawers, wastepaper baskets), open water vessels (even flower vases) or dangerous substances (alcohol, cosmetics, ink, lead, adhesives, etc).
- Screen windows and mirrors to prevent your bird flying into them.
- Switch off heaters and fans.
- Make sure other people in the house know that your parakeet is loose so that they don't suddenly open the door.
- Place newspaper underneath your parakeet's favourite perches to protect furnishings.
- Keep your parakeet well away from kitchen fumes, particularly from nonstick pans.

Time to go home

Always leave the cage door open so that your parakeet can return to it when it is ready. The first time you let your parakeet out of its cage, it is a good idea to let it find its own way back, though you can coax it with a special treat. Keep your tone of voice soft and reassuring. If your pet learns that food is available only in its cage it will soon grasp that going back in is as rewarding as coming out.

Catching a parakeet

Never try to grab hold of your parakeet or catch it while it is in flight. If your bird is hand-tame, it will perch on your finger and allow you to carry it back to its cage. If you do need to catch a bird, use a soft cloth or net, not your hand.

A hand-tame parakeet will happily come and perch on your arm.

If your parakeet is hand-tame, it will be easier to get it back into its cage. Avoid picking it up if possible, though; instead coax it back with a treat.

Cage Hygiene – for good health

A clean cage is vital if your parakeet is to remain healthy. Daily tasks can be done while your parakeet remains in its cage but once a week you will need to take it out and give the cage a thorough clean. The checklist on page 52 provides a helpful reminder of what you need to do when.

A carrying cage is useful to keep your parakeets in while you clean their cage.

You will need to replace the sand sheet in the bottom of the cage with a fresh one every week.

Cleaning kit

It is not advisable to use the same cleaning materials – bowls, cloths etc – for your parakeet as are used for the family. You will need a separate large bowl for washing food bowls, toys, etc, a scraper, a small, hard scrubbing brush and a suitable pet-safe disinfectant, which you can buy from your pet shop.

tip
Never use household detergents

Use hot water or a suitably diluted pet-safe disinfectant. Other products will be dangerous for your budgie.

SAFETY CHECKS

While you are cleaning the cage, it is a good idea to check for any damaged areas. Look out for rust, sharp edges, or splintered perches and check that the door and its catches are secure.

Daily housekeeping

Remove old food and wash food bowls thoroughly in hot water. Make sure the seed container is thoroughly dry before you refill it and place it back in the cage. Empty and refill the water bottle at the same time. You will need to remove husks from the top of the food pot regularly.

Cleaning the cage

You will need to change the sand sheet in the base of the cage every week. (If you have chosen to use loose sand for a floor covering, remove soiled sand and replace with fresh material weekly.) Check that droppings appear normal (see page 56).

Once a week, you will need to give your parakeet's cage a thorough clean. If someone else can supervise and your pet is hand-tame, you can let it

loose while you clean the cage. Alternatively, pop it into a carrying cage.

Wash the base, wash and brush down the bars, and scrub perches and toys using hot water or suitably diluted pet-safe disinfectant. Dry all items before reassembling the cage and returning its occupant. Replace chewed branches where necessary.

Occasionally, you will need to disinfect the cage, as dirt, dust, traces of food, and droppings form a breeding ground for bacteria. Do this after you have washed the cage and always rinse it thoroughly in fresh water and make sure it is completely dry afterwards.

A thorough clean-out is necessary to remove not only visible droppings and food residues but also hidden bacteria.

Routine Maintenance

Like any pet, your parakeet will be reliant on you to provide for all its needs. Your main tasks will be to maintain a healthy diet and clean its cage, but you will also need to keep a check on its claws and beak to make sure that they don't become overgrown and provide it with bathing opportunities so that its plumage remains in good shape.

It is a good idea to stick to a regular routine for cleaning your parakeet's cage, feeding it and other maintenance tasks and to make a note of what you've done when so that you don't forget when tasks are due. Keep an eye on the appearance and behavior of your parakeet, too, and make a note of any changes. If you know what is normal for your pet, you will be able to identify and deal with any problems more quickly (see pages 58–59 for more on diagnosing health problems).

As you spend time with your parakeet every day, you will get used to its normal appearance. Make a note of any change that might indicate a problem.

TASK CHECKLIST

Daily
- Empty, wash, dry, and refill food and water containers.
- Cover the cage in the evening and remove the cover in the morning.
- Check your parakeet's appearance and behavior for any signs of illness.

Weekly
- Change the sand sheet (or other floor covering).
- Clean the cage and contents using hot water (see pages 50–51).

- Replace chewed branches where necessary.
- Check toys for wear and replace if needed.
- Check that your parakeet's claws and beak have not become overgrown (see opposite).
- Fit a bird bath or spray your parakeet with a fine mist sprayer (see page 29) or let it bathe in the kitchen sink under a dripping cold tap.

Monthly/occasionally
- Clean the cage with a pet-safe disinfectant (see pages 50–51).

Perches made from branches will be of varied
width, which helps prevent pressure sores
developing on a parakeet's feet.

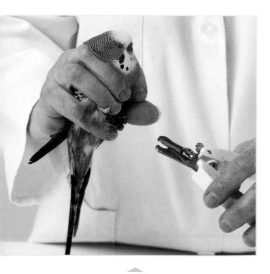

Long claws need to be clipped—a task best left to
the vet unless you have experience.

Claws and beaks

A parakeet's claws grow continuously but
are normally kept to a comfortable length
by use. If they become too long, so that
your parakeet finds it difficult to perch or
climb, you will need to get a vet to clip
them. (You can do this yourself, but you
must take care to avoid the blood vessels
in the claw.)

The beak can also become overgrown,
particularly in an old bird, if a parakeet
doesn't have enough to chew. Provide
a cuttlebone and this shouldn't be
a problem, but if your parakeet's beak does
become overgrown you will need to get
a vet to trim it.

 Provide natural branches
Branches of varied width, rather
than plastic or dowelling perches,
will help exercise your parakeet's
toes and prevent its claws from over-
growing. You can use concrete ones along
with branches.

Molting and preening

Like all birds, parakeets periodically shed their feathers and regrow new ones. Pet parakeets have no fixed molting season — a molt may be triggered by warmer temperatures (seasonal or due to central heating being turned on) or can be caused by stressful situations such as rough handling. During the molt, your pet will need a warm, quiet environment and nutritious food rich in vitamins and minerals to help it grow strong replacement feathers. Molting diets are available at most pet stores and you can see if your bird likes them.

Parakeet take great care of their plumage, cleaning and smoothing each feather with their beaks. At the same time, they waterproof their feathers by spreading an oil over them from a gland

Parakeet groom themselves fastidiously using their beaks.

situated on the lower back. In the wild, rainwater will help to keep a parakeet's feathers free of dust, but a pet bird needs opportunities to bathe to keep its feathers clean. Provide a bird bath in the cage once a week (see page 29) or spray it with water using a mister spray, directing the jet over its head.

Sleeping

Parakeet need 10–12 hours

Make a list of what you need to take as well as maintenance tasks for your friend.

A cage cover creates an artificial night for your parakeet, enabling it to extend its hours of sleep.

of sleep a night and, as with humans, a lack of sleep will make your parakeet irritable or even ill. A parakeet will stand on one leg with its head under its wing. You may need to cover your bird's cage in the evening to make sure it has enough hours of darkness.

GOING ON VACATION

Your parakeet needs daily care, so when you go on vacation you will need to find a reliable friend to care for your pet. In addition to your bird in its cage, don't forget to pack the following:

- Food – enough seed for the time you are away.
- Sand sheets – one for each week you will be away.
- Twigs – for replacement perches.
- Toys – something to play with while you are away.
- List of instructions.
- Your vet's name and telephone number.

Take your parakeet to your friend's house the day before you go away so that they can phone you if they have any questions. It would be safer to tell them not to allow your parakeet out of its cage – it can have plenty of flying time when you return from vacation.

Health Care – symptoms and cures

Few birds are easier to keep than parakeets and they are generally long-lived, but however well you care for one, it may become ill occasionally. In most cases, provided you spot symptoms quickly and take appropriate action, there is no reason why your pet should not make a full recovery. The chart on pages 58–59 will help you recognize common symptoms, but if you are in doubt as to what the problem is with your parakeet, always consult an avian vet (not all vets are familiar with birds).

A DAILY HEALTH CHECK

Make a point of checking the following daily:
- **Eyes** – should be bright and shiny.
- **Beak and nostrils** – should be bright and smooth, with no discharge from the nostrils.
- **Tail feathers** – should be sleek and clean.
- **Claws** – should not be overgrown.
- **Droppings** – should appear normal.

Spotting a sick parakeet

A generally ill parakeet should not be difficult to spot. Tell-tale signs include a general listlessness – it will be less active

Check the sand sheet for loose or discoloured droppings, a sign of illness that should never be ignored.

A carrying cage is useful for taking your budgie to see the vet. It will feel less nervous if you cover it on the journey.

than usual or than its companions – and plumage that is fluffed up and has lost its sleek appearance. Although a sick parakeet may continue to try to eat, you may notice, on closer inspection, that it has simply removed the husks from the seeds rather than eating them. (Canary seeds are darker when unhusked.) You may also notice more specific signs such as staining around the vent, discharge from the nostrils, and dull eyes.

If the vet prescribes medication for your parakeet, you can administer this in its food. Always follow recommended dosages carefully.

tip ### *Find a good avian vet*

As soon as you buy a parakeet, find your nearest avian vet so that if a problem occurs you can take your pet for treatment straight away. Parakeets can get sick very quickly and you don't want to waste valuable time.

Caring for a sick parakeet

You will need to keep a sick parakeet warm and, if it normally lives with others, to isolate it in order to assist its recovery. If your parakeet lives in a cage in a warm room, a light cover around its cage may be sufficient, but in serious cases or for an aviary bird (which you will need to move into a separate cage indoors), you can maintain a temperature of around 90°F (32°C) using an infrared lamp situated outside the cage. (You can the buy complete kit from a specialist avicultural supplier.) Some models fit easily onto the front of a breeding cage. If you have several parakeets it is worth buying a ready-made hospital cage, which can double as a quarantine cage. (Wash and disinfect the cage thoroughly after use.) Make sure that fresh seed and water is available.

You can position a millet spray within reach of your sick parakeet to tempt its appetite.

First Aid

A styptic pencil is useful for stemming minor bleeding, which can result from a torn claw or a parakeet injuring itself on something sharp. Keep your parakeet as still as possible until the bleeding has stopped. You can also apply a mild antibiotic-analgesic powder specially for birds, obtainable from a vet. If a small wound becomes infected it may form a tiny ulcer. You can cover this with tincture of iodine, which you can obtain from a pharmacist, but visit your vet if the infection does not clear up quickly.

Parakeets sometimes get seed husks or other foreign bodies in the eye. You can help your parakeet easily by diluting an eye wash 50/50 with water. Fill an eye-bath or other small container with the liquid, soak a piece of cotton wool in water, then in the liquid and squeeze it out. Hold the bird on one side and allow the liquid to dribble from the cotton ball into the bird's eye. Repeat this treatment several times a day until the eye is clear again.

DIAGNOSING AND TREATING HEALTH PROBLEMS

The health problems below are listed from most to least common.

Symptoms	Likely causes	Treatment
Loose droppings, lethargy, loss of weight	Caused by worms or bacteria, both of which can be picked up from other birds, hence the importance of quarantine and cleanliness.	Best avoided by routinely quarantining all new birds separately, and routinely cleaning all feed hoppers and cages. If an outbreak occurs, seek veterinary advice.
Long, thin parasites on feathers (only visible when wings are opened)	Feather lice	An aerosol spray or powder formulated to kill mites and lice on birds, available from your avian vet.
Snail-like tracks across the upper beak. In advanced cases, encrustations around sides of beak and on the legs.	A parasitic condition known as 'scaly face'	In mild cases, treatment is straightforward, using a lotion available at some pet stores, but if not dealt with in time, scaly face can lead to malformation of the beak and ugly legs.

Retching, mucus on the head, distended crop at base of neck	A parasitic infection known as 'sour crop'	Sour crop is relatively common in parakeets. Affected chicks may die rapidly. See an avian vet.
Prolonged and violent vomiting (not to be confused with regurgitation), sticky seeds and congested feathers on the head or around base of beak	Vomiting can be caused by a parakeet eating something that doesn't agree with it or contaminated food but may be symptomatic of a more serious complaint.	If vomiting continues for more than a day, seek veterinary assistance.
Noisy, laboured breathing, bubbly discharge from the nostrils	Respiratory infection	Seek veterinary assistance for appropriate antibiotics. (Some respiratory infections can be transmitted to humans.)
Lethargy, alteration in colour of droppings	Digestive problems (enteritis)	Your vet will prescribe a course of antiobiotics. Some forms of enteritis are infectious, so isolate the affected bird and clean its cage or aviary thoroughly.
Inflamed eye	Usually caused by a seed husk in the eye	See 'First Aid', opposite.
Swellings on the body, particularly in older birds. Weight loss, change in cere coloration	Tumor. Less common in aviary birds so may be linked to exercise. Some tumors may be caused by a virus.	External tumors (visible as swellings) may be benign (non-cancerous) and may be removed by surgery, depending on their position. Internal tumors usually prove fatal.
Feather plucking, leaving bare patches	Boredom or stress, or endo- and ectoparasites, blood, biochemical, or hormonal disorders.	Check with your vet that there is no medical cause. If not, lifestyle changes may help, but once the habit is acquired, your parakeet will find it hard to break.
Fluffed up feathers, depression, diarrhea, discharge from nares and eyes, poor appetite, rapid weight loss, and death	Chlamydiosis, or psittacosis, which can also affect cats, other animals and birds, and even people.	The disease usually proves fatal for the birds and, as it can be passed to humans, it is notifiable — i.e., your vet must tell the authorities. If caught early, it can be cured by antibiotics given in food.

Developing Your Hobby

Learning more, exhibiting parakeets, and breeding advice

Many owners of pet parakeets are content to have a single companion bird or a pair, but once you've had your new parakeet for a while, you may decide that you'd like to exhibit or breed parakeets, or perhaps be able to keep more by building an aviary. In whichever direction your interest lies, you will benefit from getting to know others who share your hobby.

Join a society

Although you can find out more about keeping parakeets by reading other books, magazines and websites, one of the best ways to do this is to join your local caged bird society (which will cater for all kinds of birds, not just parakeets) and, if you wish, your area budgerigar society.

You can find contact details of your national society on the Internet. Its secretary will be able to

put you in touch with clubs and club officials in your area. In the US, a number of magazines publish details of forthcoming club events and shows.

As well as enabling you to contact other, parakeet enthusiasts, who may have more experience in the hobby to pass on to you, parakeet clubs hold social events, host talks and slide shows and stage shows, and sales of birds.

Exhibiting parakeets

Parakeet shows, which are held at local, regional, and national levels, are great fun to visit and a good source of information.

The appearance of exhibition parakeets differs significantly from that of aviary birds and the standards set are very high. Even if you have bred parakeets, it is a good idea to visit as many shows as possible to see the physical attributes of the birds being selected by the judges before you think about entering a bird in the novice category, where you will compete with other newcomers to showing.

A prize-winning budgie – Best Spangle Green young bird at the Parakeet Society World Show – in its show case.

You will also need specialist equipment, such as electrical switches that control the lighting in the room or shed where you keep your birds in such a way as to fool the birds that spring comes in mid winter, the time of year you need to start breeding parakeets if you intend to show them. You will also need extra cages in which to keep your young birds while they molt and grow into their adult plumage, on which they are judged, and specialist show cages in which to present your birds at a show.

tip

Find a mentor

Find someone already sufficiently skilled who can teach you the ropes. The best place to meet a mentor is at a club.

Breeding Parakeets – and caring for chicks

Before you decide to breed your parakeets, it is important to make sure that you have the time and commitment necessary, as well as suitable accommodations for the breeding pair and their offspring. Perhaps most importantly, make sure that you have good homes for the babies before you begin.

Caring for breeding birds

Make sure that the parakeets that which you want to breed are healthy and tame. Parakeets can breed from as young as three months but should not be allowed to do so until they are ten or eleven months old.

In the wild, parakeets lay their eggs in holes in trees or rocks; in captivity, they need a special nest box designed for parakeets, which will attach on the outside of a breeding cage. Many commercial wood box breeding cages now come with the outside nest boxes already attached to one end of the cage. With a model that doesn't, you can simply hang the nest box on the outside front of the cage, where you will be able to examine its contents without disturbing the birds in the cage.

Sliding door

Entrance hole

Perch

Timber concave (where eggs are laid)

Sliding inspection panel

Plywood nestbox measuring 25x15x15cm (10x6x6in)

An unmated hen may lay infertile eggs. Removing them will only encourage the hen to lay more and become exhausted so it is best to leave her to incubate them uselessly. Sometimes a hen will be unable to lay an egg because it has become stuck. This condition is known as egg-binding and requires veterinary assistance.

Caring for chicks

The young chicks emerge from the eggs naked and helpless and will need special rearing food containing extra protein, called eggfood, to help them grow. Baby parakeets are fragile and should be handled only when necessary (e.g. when banding them) before they are two weeks old.

The young chicks are born naked and helpless but quickly develop feathers.

A hen can lay two or three clutches (called rounds) of five or six eggs, with the eggs laid on alternate days. The parents will need special food while laying eggs and rearing the young. The eggs will hatch at two-day intervals after 18 days' incubation. Both parents feed the young chicks, which develop quickly and are ready to leave the nest at six weeks. Once they have done so, the hen will be ready to lay again but three broods in a row is enough.

The nest box hangs on the outside front of this typical breeding cage.

From now until they leave the nest, you will need to check the chicks regularly to ensure that no dirt is stuck to their toes or inside their beaks, which can cause deformities. Soak feet in lukewarm water to loosen the dirt before picking it off carefully. Clean dirty beaks gently using a toothpick. You will also need to remove them temporarily to clean the nestbox.

At six weeks old, the baby parakeets will need to be separated from their parents to stop them disturbing the next clutch. Males and females should be separated from each other at 12 weeks old.

PROJECT TEAM

Editor: Thomas Mazorlig
Design: Patti Escabi

T.F.H. PUBLICATIONS

President/CEO: Glen S. Axelrod
Executive Vice President: Mark E. Johnson
Publisher: Christopher T. Reggio
Production Manager: Kathy Bontz

T.F.H. PUBLICATIONS, INC.

One TFH Plaza
Third and Union Avenues
Neptune City, NJ 07753